Read All About

CATS

ABYSSINIAN CATS

LYNN M. STONE

The Rourke Corporation, Inc.
Vero Beach, Florida 32964

PHOTO CREDITS
©Norvia Behling: cover, pages 9, 10, 13, 18; © Lynn M. Stone: pages 4, 6,
7, 12, 15, 16, 19, 21, 22

ACKNOWLEDGEMENTS
The author thanks Robin Sessler of Leotie Abyssinians (Mendota, IL) for
her assistance—and her cats—in the preparation of this book.

CREATIVE SERVICES:
East Coast Studios, Merritt Island, Florida

EDITORIAL SERVICES:
Janice L. Smith for Penworthy Learning Systems

Library of Congress Cataloging-in-Publication Data

Stone, Lynn M.
   Abyssinian cats / by Lynn M. Stone.
     p. cm. — (Cats)
   Includes bibliographical references (p. 24) and index.
   Summary: Describes the history, characteristics, and temperament of
the Abyssinian cat and what it is like to have one for a pet.
     ISBN 0-86593-557-2
   1. Abyssinian cat Juvenile literature. [1. Abyssinian cat. 2. Cats. 3. Pets.]
I. Title. II. Series: Stone, Lynn M.- Cats.
SF449.A28S76 1999
636.8'26—dc21
                                        99-27210
                                             CIP

Printed in the USA

TABLE OF CONTENTS

ABYSSINIAN CATS

Abyssinians are named for the African country where this **breed** (BREED), or kind, of cat originated. Abyssinia is now known as Ethiopia.

The long, lean Aby is one of the most popular **purebred** (PEUR BRED) cats in the world. It ranked fifth on a recent list published by the Cat Fanciers' Association.

One feature that sets the Aby apart from other cat breeds is its coat. All cats have fur, of course, but the Abyssinian's has a special look.

The ticked coat of the Abyssinian is one of the breed's markers.

Each hair in an Aby's coat consists of several dark bands of color. Together, these bands give the Aby's coat a ticked, or flecked, appearance.

Abyssinians have short fur, but even Abys need grooming, especially as summer approaches.

The long, lean body of the Abyssinian is typical of cats with roots in warm countries. Siamese cats also have streamlined bodies, as do several other breeds.

Abyssinians have fairly short, fine fur. Some have ear **tufts** (TUFTS) like the caracal, a wild cat of Africa.

CAT BREEDS

The Abyssinian is one of about 80 kinds of **domestic** (duh MESS tik) cats. Domestic cats are the types of cats raised by people as pets. A tiger is a cat, but it is not a domestic cat.

House cats that live away from people are called **feral** (FIR ul) cats. Feral cats live and act like wild animals.

In most cases, domestic cats have not had wild cats among their **ancestors** (AN SESS terz) for hundreds, or even thousands, of years.

This Abyssinian shares its distant ancestors with other domestic cats. The small African wildcat was one of those ancestors, dating back some 4,000 years.

Most domestic cats are not purebred. Purebreds, like the Abyssinian, are cats with parents of the same special type, or breed. The majority of domestic cats are a mix of breeds.

Most cat breeds can be distinguished from others by the shape of the cat's face and body. By itself, a cat's color is unlikely to separate it from another breed.

House cats don't really need the extra calories, but they still love to hunt. This Aby is trying to decide whether the grasshopper is dangerous.

WHAT AN ABYSSINIAN CAT LOOKS LIKE

The original Abyssinian was a reddish-brown color with darker flecks on the hairs. Since 1963, several colors have been added by cat **breeders** (BREED erz). Among those colors are red, blue, chocolate, lilac, and fawn. But don't expect to see a bright red or blue Abyssinian! Red actually refers to a light brown, while blue is a shade of gray.

These Aby kittens have the breed's original reddish-brown fur color.

This Aby kitten has light-colored "spectacles" around her eyes.

Cat breeders are people who raise cats for sale and show. They decide which female cats will mate with which male cats to produce kittens. By picking parent cats carefully, breeders can often add colors or create other changes within a breed.

Abyssinians, like other cats from warm lands, have slender, medium-sized bodies. They have large gold or green eyes. Their dark eye rims are outlined by spectacles of lighter hair. A "mascara" line reaches from each eye toward the side of the head in many Abys.

Abyssinians have small feet, fairly long legs, and large ears. Their long, slim tails are about the same length as their body.

Abys weigh from 9 to 17 pounds (4-7.5 kilograms).

Abys accept each other's company, but they don't really need it. Cats are the most independent of all domestic animals.

THE HISTORY OF ABYSSINIAN CATS

The Abyssinian cat was unknown outside of North Africa until the 1860s. At that time a few cats with the unusual ticked coats were taken from Abyssinia to England by British soldiers.

British cat breeders probably mated some of these cats with a favorite breed in England, the British shorthair.

The Abyssinian breed is most popular in North America. The breed arrived in England in the 1860s, but nearly disappeared there during World War II.

By the 1890s the Aby was an accepted breed. Abyssinians first reached the United States in 1907.

British breeders' activities were interrupted during World War II (1939-1945) and the Abyssinian nearly died out in England. Fortunately, the Aby was becoming a popular purebred cat in North America.

Abys enjoy, even demand, attention.

Abys love to poke around new things, play-hunt, and climb. The highest ledge in a room is an Aby's favorite perch.

Today the Aby enjoys its greatest popularity in North America. People like the Aby for its cool coat, but there are other reasons for owning one.

OWNING AN ABYSSINIAN

Every cat has a distinct personality. But Abyssinians are generally smart, active, and friendly pets. They're also among the most quiet cat breeds.

Because of their short fur, Abyssinians need less grooming, or fur care, than a long-haired breed.

Abyssinians like to climb, bound, and run. They often seek the highest perch in a room.

Abyssinians are social cats. They enjoy the company of people and other cats.

This Aby is being bathed with pet shampoo in the kitchen sink. Breeders do things for their cats' well-being that the animals can't do for themselves.

GLOSSARY

ancestor (AN SESS ter) — those in the past from whom a person or animal has descended; direct relatives prior to one's grandparents

breed (BREED) — a particular group of domestic animals having several of the same characteristics; a kind of domestic animal within a group of many kinds, such as a *Bengal* cat or a *Persian* cat

breeder (BREED er) — one who raises animals, such as cats, and lets them reproduce

domestic (duh MESS tik) — a type of animal that has been tamed and raised by humans for hundreds of years

feral (FIR ul) — a domestic animal that lives in the wild

purebred (PEUR BRED) — a domestic animal of a single (pure) breed

tufts (TUFTS) — long strand of fur, usually at the tips of certain animals' ears

Abys are playful without being loud. But as this cat shows, even Abys speak now and then.

23

INDEX

FURTHER READING

Find out more about Abyssinian cats and cats in general with these helpful books and information sites:

• Clutton-Brock, Juliet. *Cat.* Knopf, 1997

• Editors of Owl Magazine. *The Kids' Cat Book.* Greey de Pencier, 1990

• Evans, Mark. *ASPCA Pet Care Guide for Kids/Kittens.* Dorling Kindersley, 1992

• Scott, Carey. *Kittens.* Dorling Kindersley, 1992

• Abyssinian Cat Club of America, 4060 Croaker Lane, Woodbridge, VA 22193

• Cat Fanciers Association on line @ www.cfainc.org